Little People, BIG DREAMS
MARY SHELLEY

Written by
Mª Isabel Sánchez Vegara

Illustrated by
Yelena Bryksenkova

Frances Lincoln
Children's Books

Baby Mary was the child of two writers: a famous feminist and a well-known philosopher. She was born in London at a time of great change and amazing inventions.

But Mary's mother became ill after she was born.
The doctors couldn't do anything, and she died
when Mary was just 11 days old.

MARY
WOLLSTONECRAFT
GODWIN

Author of
A Vindication
of the rights of Woman

Born 27th April, 1759
Died 10th September, 1787

A few years later, her father married their neighbor.
When her new stepmother and children arrived at
her house, Mary knew they would not get along.

Mary had a secret retreat that she visited every day: her mother's grave at St. Pancras churchyard. There, she spent hours reading her mother's books and writing her own stories.

At night, Mary would hide behind the sofa and listen to the many artists who visited her father. One of them was a married poet named Percy Bysshe Shelley.

To everyone's surprise, Mary and Percy fell in love and ran away from London. Only Claire, Mary's stepsister, stood by their side, traveling through Europe with them.

They went to Switzerland, where they visited Lord Byron, a famous poet. It was a rainy summer, and to pass the time, Lord Byron challenged his guests to write a horror story.

Around this time, scientists discovered that the brain uses electricity to move the body. Mary was fascinated with this and thought it could be a great subject to write about.

For days, Mary busied herself with the story. One night, a terrifying image appeared in her dream: a creature made of old body parts.

The next morning, Mary began to write *Frankenstein*, the story of a monster with yellow skin and watery eyes, brought to life with an electric shock.

Mary's book became an instant success, but her name was kept secret for five years. Many people thought that such a terrifying story could only have been written by a man.

Mary kept writing all her life, but *Frankenstein* remained her best novel and the greatest horror story ever written. It became a classic, retold over and over again.

And still today, millions of readers feel a chill when they read *Frankenstein*—a story written by a fearless girl who became the mother of modern science fiction.

In Loving
Memory
of

Here Lies the

MARY SHELLEY

(Born 1797 • Died 1851)

c. 1822

c.1830

Mary Wollstonecraft Shelley (née Wollstonecraft Godwin) was born
in London at a time of great change. The world was knocking on the
door of the Industrial Revolution—a turning point in history—when
clothes and goods were no longer made by hand, but by machines.
With its many factories and working classes, London was center
stage. Here, under the watchful eye of her eccentric philosopher
father, William Godwin, Mary fell in love with books—and her
mother's writing. Although she died when Mary was just 11 days old,
her mother's passion for equality between the sexes made Mary a
brave young woman, free from the constraints of her stepmother's
rules. Well-educated for a teenage girl of the time, Mary was drawn

c. 1843–5   c. 1935

to the many philosophers, scientists, and writers who visited her
father each day. One such visitor was a poet named Percy Bysshe
Shelley, whom Mary had met in the company of his wife two years
earlier. Now at age sixteen, Mary affirmed her love for Percy and the
two eloped to begin their travels in Europe. A ghost-writing contest
on a stormy June night in 1816 inspired Mary to write *Frankenstein*.
Influenced by the experiments of physicist and philosopher Luigi
Galvani, Mary's novel weaved together scientific discoveries with
a story about the misuse of power. It became an instant classic—a
thrilling, scary story, unlike other books of the time. And just as her
mother had done years before, Mary started a revolution of her own.

Want to find out more about **Mary Shelley?**
Read one of these great books:

Mary and Frankenstein by Linda Bailey and Júlia Sardà

She Made a Monster by Lynn Fulton and Felicita Sala

BOARD BOOKS

COCO CHANEL

ISBN: 978-1-78603-245-4

MAYA ANGELOU

ISBN: 978-1-78603-249-2

FRIDA KAHLO

ISBN: 978-1-78603-247-8

AMELIA EARHART

ISBN: 978-1-78603-252-2

MARIE CURIE

ISBN: 978-1-78603-253-9

ADA LOVELACE

ISBN:978-1-78603-259-1

ROSA PARKS

ISBN: 978-1-78603-263-8

EMMELINE PANKHURST

ISBN: 978-1-78603-261-4

AUDREY HEPBURN

ISBN: 978-1-78603-255-3

ELLA FITZGERALD

ISBN:978-1-78603-257-7

BOX SETS

WOMEN IN ART

ISBN: 978-1-78603-428-1

WOMEN IN SCIENCE

ISBN: 978-1-78603-429-8

BOOKS & PAPER DOLLS

EMMELINE PANKHURST
ISBN: 978-1-78603-400-7

MARIE CURIE
ISBN: 978-1-78603-401-4

Collect the
Little People, **BIG DREAMS** series:

FRIDA KAHLO

ISBN: 978-1-84780-783-0

COCO CHANEL

ISBN: 978-1-84780-784-7

MAYA ANGELOU

ISBN: 978-1-84780-889-9

AMELIA EARHART

ISBN: 978-1-84780-888-2

AGATHA CHRISTIE

ISBN: 978-1-84780-960-5

MARIE CURIE

ISBN: 978-1-84780-962-9

ROSA PARKS

ISBN: 978-1-78603-018-4

AUDREY HEPBURN

ISBN: 978-1-78603-053-5

EMMELINE PANKHURST
ISBN: 978-1-78603-020-7

ELLA FITZGERALD

ISBN: 978-1-78603-087-0

ADA LOVELACE
ISBN: 978-1-78603-076-4

JANE AUSTEN
ISBN: 978-1-78603-120-4

GEORGIA O'KEEFFE

ISBN: 978-1-78603-122-8

HARRIET TUBMAN
ISBN: 978-1-78603-227-0

ANNE FRANK
ISBN: 978-1-78603-229-4

MOTHER TERESA

ISBN: 978-1-78603-230-0

JOSEPHINE BAKER
ISBN: 978-1-78603-228-7

L. M. MONTGOMERY

ISBN: 978-1-78603-233-1

JANE GOODALL

ISBN: 978-1-78603-231-7

SIMONE DE BEAUVOIR

ISBN: 978-1-78603-232-4

MUHAMMAD ALI
ISBN: 978-1-78603-331-4

STEPHEN HAWKING

ISBN: 978-1-78603-333-8

MARIA MONTESSORI
ISBN: 978-1-78603-755-8

VIVIENNE WESTWOOD

ISBN: 978-1-78603-757-2

MAHATMA GANDHI

ISBN: 978-1-78603-787-9

DAVID BOWIE

ISBN: 978-1-78603-332-1

WILMA RUDOLPH

ISBN: 978-1-78603-751-0

DOLLY PARTON

ISBN: 978-1-78603-760-2

BRUCE LEE

ISBN: 978-0-7112-4629-4

RUDOLF NUREYEV

ISBN: 978-1-78603-791-6

ZAHA HADID

ISBN: 978-0-7112-4641-6

MARY SHELLEY
ISBN: 978-0-7112-4639-3

Brimming with creative inspiration, how-to projects, and useful information to enrich your everyday life, Quarto Knows is a favorite destination for those pursuing their interests and passions. Visit our site and dig deeper with our books into your area of interest: Quarto Creates, Quarto Cooks, Quarto Homes, Quarto Lives, Quarto Drives, Quarto Explores, Quarto Gifts, or Quarto Kids.

First Published in the UK in 2019 by Frances Lincoln Children's Books, an imprint of The Quarto Group.

400 First Avenue North, Suite 400, Minneapolis, MN 55401, USA.

T (612) 344-8100 F (612) 344-8692 www.QuartoKnows.com

First Published in Spain in 2019 under the title Pequeña & Grande Mary Shelley

by Alba Editorial, s.l.u., Baixada de Sant Miquel, 1, 08002 Barcelona

www.albaeditorial.es

A catalog record for this book is available from the British Library.

ISBN 978-1-78603-748-0

Set in Futura BT.

Published by Rachel Williams • Designed by Karissa Santos

Edited by Katy Flint • Production by Jenny Cundill

Manufactured in Guangdong, China CC072019

9 7 5 3 1 2 4 6 8

Photographic acknowledgments (pages 28–29, from left to right) 1. Miniature of Mary Shelley painted posthumously, after 1822 © The Bodleian Library, University of Oxford, Shelley relics (d) 2. Portrait identified as Mary Shelley, 1843–5 © The Bodleian Library, University of Oxford, Shelley relics 39 3. Mary Wollstonecraft Shelley, 1830 © Hulton Archive / Stringer via Getty Images 4. Boris Karloff as The Monster in *Frankenstein*, c. 1935 © Archive Photos / Stringer via Getty Images